THE LABOR MOVEMENT
IN THE UNITED STATES

ECONOMICS FOR TODAY

THE LABOR MOVEMENT IN THE UNITED STATES

John J. Flagler

Series Editor: M. Barbara Killen
Professor, University of Minnesota

Lerner Publications Company ■ Minneapolis, Minnesota

To my mentor, Dr. Virgil C. Crisafulli

Words that appear in **bold** type are listed in a glossary that starts on page 106.

Library of Congress Cataloging-in-Publication Data

Flagler, John J.
   The labor movement in the United States / John J. Flagler.
     p.   cm. — (Economics for today)
   Summary: Traces the history of organized labor in the United States and discusses its influence on the society.
   ISBN 0-8225-1778-7 (lib. bdg.)
   1. Trade-unions—United States—History—Juvenile literature.
[1. Labor and laboring classes.] I. Title. II. Series.
HD6508.25.F57   1990
331.88'0973—dc20   89-36242
                                               CIP
                                               AC

Manufactured in the United States of America

1 2 3 4 5 6 7 8 9 10 99 98 97 96 95 94 93 92 91 90

UPPER MIDWEST LOCAL 1M

CONTENTS

INTRODUCTION

The lives of working people in the United States have improved dramatically from the early factory system through the Industrial Revolution to the modern technological society. The reasons why workers organize today, however, remain essentially the same. Workers organize to exert some measure of control over their own lives. They organize to resist being "lost in the shuffle"— becoming merely a number in a computer file, a cog in some huge, impersonal machine. Workers organize as a response to decisions by employers that affect their lives and their families.

The question is not whether there will continue to be a labor movement in the United States. That issue has long since been settled. Rather, the question is this: What kind of labor movement can be developed that will contribute best to both the health of the nation's economy and to the strength of its society?

HOW IT ALL BEGAN

Some historians mistakenly trace the origin of the modern labor union to the medieval **guild**. Actually, workingmen's guilds were organizations set up during the Middle Ages in Europe by groups of **master craftsmen** to regulate commerce, or business, in their trade areas. The guilds determined such matters as the standards of acceptable craftwork, the length of time an **apprentice** would serve before working on his own, and the prices of products.

At "bell time," workers leave a 19th-century New England factory.

A stone mason and a carpenter demonstrate their skills for a guild official. Guilds operated much like modern trade associations.

These guilds more nearly resembled trade associations like those formed today by auto dealers, funeral directors, retail grocers, and hardware dealers— relatively small business ventures. Trade associations, like the old guilds, are self-governing groups of businesspeople concerned with how business is practiced in their field.

Labor unions, by contrast, developed in the United States in the early 1800s with the breakdown of the "cottage industries." The term **cottage industries** refers to the production of goods—furniture, shoes, pottery, or hardware, for example—by a craftsman working out of his own home. Sometimes the cottage industry was run by women—seamstresses, bakers, milliners, and herbalists. More often, cottage industries were male-dominated, small businesses.

The Apprenticeship System

Cottage industries relied on the apprenticeship system for workers. Under that system, a boy became an apprentice to a master craftsman to learn a trade. The apprentice lived with the master craftsman's family while completing several years of **indentured service**, or work in exchange for training and room and board. After long years of training, the young men became **journeymen**. Journeymen traveled around, working for different craftsmen, until they saved enough money to open their own shops as master craftsmen.

Often a master craftsman had a shed or shop attached to his family's living quarters. There, he and his apprentices made articles which they sold in their town. They usually produced only as many items as were ordered, or "bespoken," by the local townspeople and nearby farm families.

This pattern of working life started to change in the United States in the early 1800s, when families began moving from the East across the Appalachian Mountains in large numbers. The pioneers and settlers who moved westward were mostly farmers, trappers, and traders looking for a better life in the new lands. Craftsmen, on the other hand, tended to remain in the East. The demand, or market, for their wares was growing because of the expanding population in the original colonies.

This separation between the westward-moving pioneer population and the eastern sources of goods and supplies brought upon the stage a figure some historians call the merchant capitalist, or "Yankee Trader." Originally he plied his trade in a covered wagon, and his

A Yankee Trader shows off his wagonful of wares to a colonial family.

arrival in a frontier settlement was announced by the banging and clanging of iron pans and kettles.

He was the original middleman who purchased finished goods from craftsmen on the East Coast for as little as he could and sold the goods in frontier outposts for as much as he could get. He eventually expanded his business by selling his wares to general stores.

Meanwhile, the pool of journeymen and young apprentices in the East increased steadily. America was being populated by the poor—in the words of the Privy

Council of England, "rogues, vagabonds, and sturdy beggars." Waves of immigrants sought to escape poverty by learning a craft, and the apprenticeship system flourished.

Birth of the Factory System

Master craftsmen, who had formerly set their own prices, now began to compete against each other, since Yankee Traders bought goods from the shop with the lowest prices. As each shop strived to offer the lowest price, the prices of all finished goods fell. The masters responded by producing more goods. They expanded their shops, hiring more journeymen and taking in more apprentices from among new immigrants.

With each passenger ship that docked in an Eastern seaport, however, the ranks of poor immigrants seeking work grew faster than did the available jobs. The newly arriving workers had no choice but to compete vigorously against each other for jobs. Because so many people were available for work, masters could pay lower wages. At the same time, masters were lengthening working hours and turning out products faster.

This combination of circumstances soon led to the creation of large shops with many journeymen and apprentices employed by the master craftsman. He, in turn, often borrowed money to expand the shop and to purchase supplies and tools. With these developments, the factory system in the U.S. was born. The growth of the early factory system permanently altered the relationship between the employer and the work force. The "one big happy family" of the colonial workshop had passed into history.

The evolution of the factory system: Above, a handful of artisans working together make up this colonial factory in Boston in 1766. Below, by 1877, factories had become huge places that employed hundreds of workers.

Early Unions

In the face of increased production, long working hours, and declining wages, small groups of workers began to band together for protection from what they saw as intolerable working conditions. Colonial chronicles report incidents of workers "standing out"—refusing to report for work—when they learned that their employer had increased their work quota, lengthened their workday, or lowered their wage.

This early form of **strike** occasionally resulted in a one-time negotiation to modify the employer's unpopular decision. Long-term employment agreements rarely issued from such actions, however. More often, the strike failed, because the unhappy workers could be replaced so easily from the ever-swelling ranks of new immigrants. Further, the courts treated the organized grouping of workers as a criminal conspiracy to restrain trade, and the leaders of protests were often jailed.

The law was more accepting of workers who bonded together in "benevolent societies" to ensure their members of visitations at their sick bed, a decent burial, and concern for their widows and orphans. Many of these benevolent societies of working people later developed into full-fledged labor unions with broad programs designed to improve the lot of workers.

WORKING AND LIVING CONDITIONS IN THE "GOOD OLD DAYS"

We tend to romanticize the past. Prints such as those by Currier and Ives portray life in early America through graceful images of prosperous families in stylish finery. They are shown driving horse-drawn sleighs through crisp winter scenes to imposing homesteads on snow-covered hills, or enjoying summer picnics beside a clear stream in lush countryside. Black slaves were often portrayed in art as merry folk, singing and dancing at a holiday gathering in the shadow of a spectacular mansion.

A handful of artists, writers, and poets painted quite a different picture of the "good old days," however. Charles Dickens wrote of the abysmal poverty of working people in England. In the U.S., Harriet Beecher Stowe dramatized the truer face of slavery in her 1852 novel *Uncle Tom's Cabin.* Black writers and poets like Frederick Douglass and Sojourner Truth portrayed the harsh realities of being black in 19th-century United States.

To understand the birth of the labor movement, it is helpful to reflect on what life was really like for workers and their families.

During the infancy of the factory system, most work was done by indentured servants and low-paid journeymen. Black slaves toiled on the plantations of the South. Child labor was common.

Under the yoke of slavery, blacks toiled long hours in the fields.

During the 19th century, the slums of New York City teemed with immigrants from Europe. They gave their crowded neighborhoods names like Hell's Kitchen and Bone Alley.

So-called **free workers**, who were not part of the apprenticeship system, labored 80 hours a week for pitifully low wages. In the eastern cities, butchers earned 33 cents a day in 1786, and carpenters worked 14 to 16 hours a day for 50 cents. As oppressive as these conditions were, workers' living standards declined even further after the spread of the factory system in the early 19th century.

An economic recession called the panic of 1837 caused a general lowering of wages at a time when prices of essential goods rose rapidly. The distress worsened as the heaviest waves of immigration in history reached the New World. By mid-century, the wave crested at over 500,000 persons a year, with the majority of new immigrants crowding into the slums of large eastern cities.

Living conditions for immigrant families in cities were appalling. After long hours working on the docks, in crowded factories, and in smelly packinghouses, men, women, and children returned to run-down buildings where whole families often lived in one or two rooms. The names these working people gave to their tenement neighborhoods reflected the anger and despair that they felt: Hell's Kitchen, Bandit's Roost, the Bottoms, Kerosene Row, Bone Alley, and Shantytown.

Between 1843 and 1850, the cost of food increased 50 percent, while wages fell steadily, according to the abolitionist Horace Greeley. In 1851 he estimated that a family of five would need a weekly income of $10.37 for the minimum necessities of life. At the time, only skilled workers like carpenters and bricklayers were making $10 a week. Wages in textile mills were $3 a week for women and $5 for men.

At these low wage levels it was necessary for everyone in a family to work, just to survive. Children worked in factories, mills, retail shops, and even mines.

Industrial homework was a common practice of the day. Workers would carry parcels of work materials home to their tenement "flats," where work continued after the evening meal. The family would sit around the dinner table sewing buttons on garments, hand-rolling cigars, or filling small packets with spices or medicine. The finished goods would be returned to the employer in the morning for payment by the piece—often, mere pennies for goods that sold for many times the cost of labor and materials.

The whole family gathers around the table to sew garments. Industrial homework was common in the late 19th century. The families sometimes earned only pennies for each piece sewn.

Factory Working Conditions

Working in the factories was dangerous, because employers often neglected even simple safety precautions. One tragic industrial accident was a fire in the Triangle Shirt Waist Factory in New York City in 1911. The factory bosses kept the doors locked, because they worried that the workers would steal. When the fire broke out, getting out of the burning factory was nearly impossible. The fire took the lives of 154 workers, most of them young women and children. One young woman, Rosie Safran, gave this account of the tragedy:

> I heard somebody cry "Fire!" I left everything and ran for the door on the Washington Place side. The door was locked and immediately there was a great jam of girls before it. The fire was on the other side, driving us away from the only door that the bosses had left open for us to use in going in or out. They had the doors locked all the time.
>
> The fire had started on our floor, and quick as I had been in getting to the Washington Place door, the flames were already blazing fiercely and spreading fast. If we couldn't get out we would all be roasted alive. The locked door that blocked us was half of wood; the upper half was thick glass. Some girls were screaming, some were beating the door with their fists, some were trying to tear it open. Someone broke out the glass part of the door with something hard and heavy, I suppose the head of a machine, and I climbed or was pulled through the broken glass and ran downstairs to the sixth floor, where someone took me down to the street.
>
> I got out to the street and watched the upper floors burning, and the girls hanging by their hands and then dropping as the fire reached up to them. There they were dead on the sidewalk. It was an awful, awful sight, especially to me who had so many friends among the girls and young men who were being roasted alive or dashed to death.

In spite of low wages and filthy and dangerous working conditions, immigrants competed for jobs. There were never enough jobs to meet the demand. The sociologist and author Robert Hunter described the steel districts of Chicago in 1904:

> On cold, rainy mornings, at the dusk of dawn, I

have been awakened, two hours before my rising time, by the monotonous clatter of hobnailed boots on the plank sidewalks, as the procession to the factory passed under my window. Heavy, brooding men; tired, anxious women; thinly dressed unkempt little girls, and frail, joyless lads passed along, half awake, not one uttering a word, as they hurried to the great factory. . . . Hundreds of others, obviously a hungrier, poorer lot . . . waited in front of a closed gate until finally a great red-bearded man came out and selected twenty-three of the strongest, best looking of the men. For these the gates were opened, and the others, with downcast eyes, marched off to seek employment elsewhere or to sit at home, or in a saloon, or in a lodging house. . . .

Lives of the Wealthy

The workers' sense of the injustice of their working and living conditions was deepened by their awareness of how the very wealthy lived. In _The Big Change. . . 1900–1950_, Frederick Lewis Allen describes the homes of some wealthy Americans:

. . . Frederick W. Vanderbilt's great house at Hyde Park, in which the dining room was approximately 50 feet long; . . . William K. Vanderbilt's Idle Hour at Oakdale—with 110 rooms, 45 bathrooms, and a garage ready to hold 100 automobiles. But the champion of all the turn-of-the-century chateaux was George W. Vanderbilt's ducal palace at Asheville, North Carolina, which he called Biltmore. . . . It had 40 master bedrooms, a Court of Palms, an Oak Drawing Room, a Banqueting Hall, a Print Room, a Tapestry Gallery, and a Library with 250,000 volumes. It was surrounded by an estate which . . . covered 203 square miles.

*John D. Rockefeller was born the son of a peddler and became the
richest man in the world during his lifetime. He made his fortune in
the oil business, organizing the Standard Oil Company.*

In one year, Vanderbilt employed more men and spent
more money on his hobby of landscape gardening and
wildlife management than the Department of Agriculture spent on the needs of all the farmers in the United
States, according to Frederick Lewis Allen.

Historians have depicted John D. Rockefeller as a man
of notoriously frugal habits—his standard tip for any service was a dime. Allen describes his estate at Poncan-
tico Hills as containing

> . . . more than 75 buildings . . . Within his estate
> were 75 miles of private roads on which he could take
> his afternoon drive; a private golf links on which he

could play his morning game; and anywhere from 1,000 to 1,500 employees, depending on the season.

    . . . Rockefeller also owned an estate at Lakewood, which he occupied in the spring; an estate at Ormond Beach in Florida for his winter use; a townhouse . . . in New York; an estate at Forest Hill, Cleveland, which he did not visit; and a house on Euclid Avenue in Cleveland, likewise unused by him.

Concludes Allen, "Never, perhaps, did any man live a more frugal life on a more colossal scale."

The extravagance of the wealthy was eagerly reported to anyone who had the price of a three-cent newspaper. In 1900 Andrew Carnegie enjoyed a personal income of close to $80 million in current dollars, with no income tax to pay. This compared to a worker's average annual income of about $1,500 at the time, measured in current dollars.

Such disparities between the lives of the upper class and those of the working class contributed to the birth of the labor movement.

CHILD LABOR

To understand how unions grew, imagine yourself in the place of a young person in the days when full-time work was commonly performed by children. The following description of work in a coal mine in Pennsylvania appeared in the *Labor Standard* on May 17, 1879. It may give you better insight into the conditions that gave rise to the modern labor movement.

In these works 300 men and boys are employed; and when I went through the buildings and through the mine I saw them all. Among all these 300, although I was with them for hours, I did not hear a laugh or even see a smile.

In a little room in this big, black shed—a room not twenty feet square—where a broken stove, red hot, tries vainly to warm the cold air that comes in through the open window, forty boys are picking their lives away. The floor of the room is an inclined plane, and a stream of coal pours constantly in from some unseen place above, crosses the room and pours out again into some unseen place below.

Rough board seats stretch across the room, five or six rows of them, very low and very dirty, and on these the boys sit, and separate the slate from the coal as it runs down the inclined plane. . . .

These little fellows go to work in this cold, dreary room at seven o'clock in the morning and work till it is too dark to see any longer. For this they get $1 to $3 a week. One result of their work is clean, free coal, that burns away to ashes in the grate; another result I found in a little miner's graveyard, beside a pretty little church, where more than every other stone bears the name of some little fellow under fifteen years of age.

Not three boys in this roomful could read or write. Shut in from everything that is pleasant, with no chance to learn, with no knowledge of what is going on about them, with nothing to do but work, grinding their little lives away in this dusty room, they are no more than the wire screens that separate the great lumps of coal from the small. They have no games; when their day's work is done they are too tired for that. They know nothing but the difference between slate and coal.

The disgrace of child labor spanned both factory and farm and persisted well into the 1930s. The main reason child labor was used was that kids worked cheap. Cynical employers often asked "Why hire a man for a buck when you can get a kid for a dime?"

A child factory worker. Many children started working in factories, mills, or mines before they were 10 years old. They didn't get the chance to go to school.

It is more difficult to understand the social attitudes that permitted child labor to flourish for more than a century. Workers tended to accept child labor as something they were powerless to change. So deeply embedded in the fabric of national life was child labor that it went largely unnoticed in the press; it was not considered newsworthy. Social reformers occasionally succeeded in raising the issue, but nothing was done to change the situation.

Opposition to reform proved formidable. In 1883

A young girl works in a textile mill. The textile mills depended heavily on child labor.

Charles Harding, president of the Merchants Woolen Company, told a congressional committee investigating child labor: "There is such a thing as too much education for working people sometimes. I have seen cases where young people are spoiled for labor by . . . too much refinement."

No laws limiting the use of child labor resulted from this congressional investigation. Although some states began to pass laws curtailing the practice, in 1910 nearly two million children were working in factories, mills, and mines, as well as on farms.

In 1919 Congress required firms that employed children to pay a special tax. This attempt to use federal taxes to restrict child labor was declared unconstitutional. A 1924 effort to prohibit child labor by Constitutional amendment also failed.

It was not until 1935 that a child labor law passed. The Walsh-Healy Act forbade employment of boys under age 16 and girls under 18 on work performed for the federal government. This law was followed in 1938 by the Fair Labor Standards Act, which extended the ban on child labor to most occupations.

The frustrations workers faced in trying to curb the exploitation of children revealed the weakness of the labor movement. Against the odds, however, immigrant workers kept organizing unions.

4

IMMIGRANTS AND THE LABOR MOVEMENT

Human nature never really changes. People of an earlier time had similar goals and hopes to those of the men, women, and youth of today. Most people want freedom from poverty and the opportunity to grow, to become what they want to be. The United States was founded by people who believed that the New World offered political, religious, and economic freedom.

They came in enormous waves, usually by the cheapest passage available. A seemingly endless stream of immigrants left the cramped ship compartments where they had eaten, slept,

prayed, and sang, living for weeks at a time on storm-
tossed seas. Whole families came down the gangplanks,
meager possessions slung over shoulders, often with
babies in their arms.

While the saga of the European immigrants continues to inspire their children, grandchildren, and great-
grandchildren, who make up the majority of Americans,
other immigrations were more grim. African Americans
trace their ancestry to the atrocities of the slave trade.
Sold into captivity by stronger tribes or betrayed by corrupt leaders, many thousands of shackled Africans were
transported in the holds of filthy slave-trading vessels
to work in the plantation fields of the Southland.

Very few slaves made their way to freedom in the North.

*Many immigrants traveled in steerage, the cheapest section of a ship.
Each partition in steerage, often no more than 10 feet long and 3 feet
high, was home to 6 to 10 people for at least 40 days.*

An auctioneer takes bids for a slave.

Not until after the Civil War did black people begin to disperse from the rural work force to seek jobs in industry. Many black people had gained important skills operating and maintaining farm equipment, building their own shelter, and making their own clothing. Most, however, were relatively unskilled at industrial tasks and had to take jobs at the bottom of the economic ladder.

Many Asian Americans immigrated at about the same time as the largest groups of European immigrants. Huge numbers of Chinese Americans worked at the hazardous job of building railroads through the West. Thousands of low-paid laborers died from the demanding work of

More than 15,000 Chinese workers helped to build the Northern Pacific Railway, which stretched from Minnesota to the Pacific coast.

laying new rail lines through mountain passes and across arid deserts. Japanese immigrants, on the other hand, more commonly were employed as farm workers in the orchards, fields, and vineyards of California and Oregon.

As generations of Asian Americans found more skilled jobs and broader opportunities, their jobs in the fields and on the railroads were filled by Mexican immigrants in the West. A similar immigration of other Hispanics, many from Puerto Rico and Cuba, occurred in the East.

At the same time, Native Americans left reservations in increasing numbers to pursue the promise of a better life in the cities. Like the immigrants, Native Americans new to the industrial world usually found that jobs were scarce and poorly paid.

The period of the greatest immigration peaked shortly after the turn of the 20th century. Almost 500,000 people arrived in 1900. The record level reached 1.3 million immigrants in 1907. Laws passed after World War I cut the immigrant flow to a relative trickle thereafter.

The rise of organized labor in the United States was tied to the values and life-styles of immigrant workers. The great immigrations closely coincided with the period of the U.S. Industrial Revolution—the development and rapid expansion of steam- and electric-powered machinery. The Industrial Revolution gave birth to a production system based on large factories, which relied on complex machinery and often employed hundreds, even thousands, of workers in a single location.

The Changing Work Ethic

A society's attitude about the meaning and importance of work is called its work ethic. In colonial America, the predominant work ethic exalted the virtue of hard work as a means to spiritual salvation. The so-called Protestant work ethic held that economic success was a divine reward for a good person's thrift and industry. In contrast, poverty was a sign of divine displeasure with a person's sinfulness and laziness.

This ethic led to a widely held belief that a person with wealth and status also had moral superiority. During a miners' strike in 1902, George Baer, a spokesman for the coal industry, told Theodore Roosevelt: "The rights and interests of the laboring man will be protected and cared for, not by the labor agitators, but by the Christian men to whom God in his infinite wisdom has given control of the property interests of this country."

The Protestant work ethic posed a stubborn philosophical barrier to workers' organizations. Many immigrant workers, who had been accustomed to a philosophy that valued cooperation and **collective action**, were puzzled by the belief that competition produced wealth and wealth meant moral superiority.

With the arrival of successive waves of immigrants, a new work ethic emerged. Whether they came from Europe or Asia, these workers valued the welfare of the family. Like the colonial Americans, later immigrants worked hard, but not primarily to gain spiritual salvation. They worked so their children would have a better life. Workers generally understood that they would remain in the working class, but that their children might move up to the middle class or better.

The first generation of immigrant workers sought to improve their living and working conditions through trade unions and political action. With its focus on group action, the emerging immigrant work ethic was on a collision course with the rugged individualism embraced by the middle class and the wealthy in the United States.

The right of workers to speak up as a group about their wages and working conditions posed a threat to the owners of the factories, railroads, and mines. It raised the issue of property versus personal rights, a conflict that has never been neatly resolved.

Employers firmly opposed the growth of the labor movement in the United States. They mounted formidable economic, legal, and even private police forces to oppose the unionization of their workers. For over a century, battles were fought on **picket lines** and in the courts before a federal labor policy encouraging free **collective bargaining** was adopted by Congress.

LABOR AND THE LAW

Before 1935, the story of labor and the law is one of almost unbroken repression. The early U.S. legal system was based on early English common law doctrines, which encouraged the growth of commerce by removing any obstacles to the making of profit. When U.S. workers tried to organize, they found that this legal tradition was a major roadblock to their success.

Many early workers' associations were formed as benevolent societies, providing burial expenses for deceased members and income assistance to their needy families. Some associations,

however, began activities to protect the job interests of craftsmen. One way the craftsmen did this was to agree among themselves on a "bill of prices" for their labor. They then refused to work for any employer who offered lower wages than the stated minimum.

In Philadelphia in 1786, this kind of agreement resulted in the nation's first significant strike. Printers struck to demand a minimum wage of $1 a day. There were no written labor agreements in those days, but the strike appears to have succeeded. The printers soon returned to work for higher wages.

The next important strike in Philadelphia, five years later, sought to prevent wage reductions and to establish a standard 12-hour workday. (The average workday at the time was 14 hours.) The strike resolution bound journeymen carpenters "by the sacred ties of honour" to stand together "that, in the future, a day's work, amongst us, shall be deemed to commence at six o'clock in the morning, and terminate at six in the evening of each day."

These small victories in Philadelphia encouraged other craftsmen to form societies in Boston, New York, Baltimore, and Pittsburgh. Most of these early unions were short-lived, however. Their attempt to establish standard wages and hours—personal rights—conflicted with the law, which protected employers' property—property rights.

The Criminal Conspiracy Doctrine

The earliest legal doctrine affecting unions in the U.S. was laid out in the *Commonwealth v. Journeymen*

Cordwainers case in 1806. (The term "cordwainer" meant leatherworkers, most of whom were boot and shoemakers.) The indictment against eight shoemakers read in part: ". . . the prisoners are charged with attempting to increase and augment the wages paid them and for deceitfully forming themselves into a club to attain their ends, thus constituting a criminal conspiracy."

The judge read the following instructions to the jury: "A combination of workmen to raise their wages may be considered from a twofold point of view; one is to benefit themselves . . . the other is to injure those who do not join their society. The rule of law condemns both." The jury delivered a verdict of guilty as charged, and the eight shoemakers were fined and forbidden from engaging in any further activities that would restrict the "free flow of trade."

The criminal conspiracy doctrine presented a barrier to any effective trade union action. It was finally lifted, a generation later, by the _Commonwealth v. Hunt_ decision in 1842. Justice Lemuel Shaw of Massachusetts ruled in the _Hunt_ decision that it was not unlawful for workers to peaceably associate in unions to improve their lot. The _Hunt_ decision, however, limited the ways they could attain their goals. Strikes and organized refusals to work for unfair employers (**boycotts**) were still held to be illegal.

Industrial Warfare: The Law of the Bomb and the Gallows

Workers responded to the legal restraints on their **right of free association** by forming workers' political parties during the first half of the 19th century. The typical

William Sylvis was the brilliant leader of the National Labor Union.

party platform, or set of goals, included a 10-hour work-day, free public education, ending imprisonment for debt, and the legal right to form unions.

These local parties in Philadelphia, New York, and Boston never achieved the status of a national political organization. Nevertheless, they were an important influence on the Democratic Party during the terms of presidents Andrew Jackson and Martin Van Buren.

Workers also tried to organize local unions into some kind of a national federation. The first such organization, the National Labor Union, survived only six years. Its leader was William Sylvis, the head of the Iron Molders Union and a brilliant writer and speaker.

Founded in 1866, the National Labor Union ventured into politics, helping form the National Labor Union and Reform Party. After repeated defeats of their candidates

In the middle of a snowstorm, hundreds of women shoe workers in Lynn, Massachusetts, marched to protest their low wages.

at the polls, the federation and the party dissolved in 1872.

Defeats on the picket line, in the courts, and at the polling places sometimes provoked frustrated working people to militant action. A near-riot broke out during a strike parade in Lynn, Massachusetts, in March 1860. Strikers—mostly women and children shoe workers—were pelted with snowballs by onlookers. Many shoe workers later joined the picketing, and the strike succeeded in gaining higher wages from the employers.

Sympathetic farmers and unorganized workers joined strikers across the country. They increasingly relied on mass picketing to press their demands. What followed was an era of violence and repression more ferocious than any experienced by other labor movements in the Western world.

In 1874 the coal operators of Pennsylvania broke a contract they had with the coal workers' union by ordering a wage cut. Coal workers responded by refusing to work, thus closing the mines. Their strike came to be known as the "Long Strike" of 1875. The operators brought in **strikebreakers** and organized a paid militia known as the "coal and iron police" to force the opening of the mines. A shooting war broke out and spread to surrounding states.

Many of the coal miners were Irish. A rumor spread that acts of terrorism were being committed by an Irish secret society commonly known as the "Molly Maguires." An undercover detective joined the group and collected evidence leading to the arrest of 24 men, who were then convicted. Ten of them were hanged, while the rest were given long jail sentences.

Historians disagree about how active the Molly Maguires were in the Long Strike. It is agreed, however, that the harsh outcome of the trial succeeded in breaking the miners' spirit and crushing the strike. Unionism in mining was virtually dead for the next generation.

The news of labor disputes during the decade following the Long Strike reads like a war bulletin. In 1877 a group of railroad workers rioted in Martinsburg, West Virginia, after their wages were cut. Twelve were killed and scores were wounded. In Pittsburgh, a force of 650 federal militiamen was dispatched to quiet an unruly mob after the state militia had joined the strikers. Much property was destroyed, and casualties ran high on both sides.

Terence Powderly was an important labor leader during the late 1800s. He helped reconcile differences between the Knights of Labor and the newly formed American Federation of Labor.

A second attempt to establish a national federation of unions had been begun in 1869 with the founding of the Knights of Labor under Uriah Stephens, a tailor and a gifted speaker. He retired in 1879. He was succeeded by Terence V. Powderly, a railroad worker turned lawyer and the mayor of Scranton, Pennsylvania. Under Powderly's leadership, the Noble Order of the Knights of Labor became the dominant labor force of the 1880s, organizing some 700,000 workers. Their aims included an eight-hour workday and one big union for all workers, skilled and unskilled.

The early labor federations were weak organizations. After losing some important strike battles, membership in the Knights of Labor rapidly declined. Perhaps the event that signaled the end of the Knights most dramatically was what was known as "the Haymarket Riot."

The riot in Haymarket Square spelled doom for the Knights of Labor. Four men, who were later proved innocent, were hanged in connection with the incident.

The event began when four workers were shot at the Chicago plant of the McCormick International Harvester Company in May 1886. At a protest meeting held in Haymarket Square, a bomb was thrown, killing a policeman. In the panic that followed, 180 policemen opened fire on the crowd, killing 10 and wounding hundreds. Widespread arrests were made, and a trial was held. Public opinion turned against labor as newspapers whipped up hysteria towards the "anarchists." Although no proof was given that they had thrown the bomb, four workmen were hanged.

Six years later, the men were proved innocent. It was too late for those who had been executed. It was also too late for the Knights of Labor, who had dwindled away. In 1893 Powderly resigned as the Grand Master Workman, marking the end of the Knights of Labor.

Founding of the AFL

In 1886 a new force in the labor movement, the American Federation of Labor, emerged. The AFL was founded by skilled workers in various trades, members of a handful of struggling **craft unions**. From the beginning, the federation worked under vigorous leadership. Its first president was Samuel Gompers, an immigrant cigarmaker who had entered the shops at the age of 13. He gained much of his early education on the job by serving as a reader, a union-paid worker who read aloud to others working in the shop.

Samuel Gompers believed that workers and their families could achieve a better life only through collective action—that "the rising tide lifts all boats." Gompers charted a careful course for the AFL, adopting a practical program, later to be called "job-conscious" unionism. Gompers's program was devoted to improving wages, hours, and working conditions through peaceful collective bargaining.

The AFL was successful in organizing craft unions across the country. By the turn of the century, the federation had almost 600,000 members. In spite of the nonpolitical character of the AFL, unionism continued to face hostility from employers. The employers were now using a new weapon to frustrate the growth of the labor movement—the **injunction**.

Injunctions are court orders forbidding certain actions. Employers would ask the court for injunctions forbidding unions to strike or to organize workers in a particular factory or industry. Injunctions could be secured from any court with remarkable ease. The still-prevailing English common law doctrine valued

Samuel Gompers started his labor career as a cigarmaker and went on to lead the American Federation of Labor. His program of "job-conscious" unionism proved successful and enduring.

property over human rights. If an employer claimed that a strike represented a danger to his property, he could have an injunction issued promptly. Often granted without the judge even hearing the unions' arguments, the injunction proved a serious obstacle to the growth and effectiveness of unions.

Craft unions did continue to grow slowly under Gompers's leadership of the AFL. But steel, railroads, and other basic industries repeatedly crushed their workers' attempts to organize any industrial union. (An **industrial union** includes all workers in a particular industry, regardless of their level of skills.)

Employers also used the **yellow-dog contract** to prevent union organization. The yellow-dog contract was an agreement that a worker signed when hired, stating that he or she would not join a union. Employees who refused to sign the contract were fired; prospective employees had to sign in order to be hired. A union that tried to recruit a worker who had signed a yellow-dog contract could be sued for interfering with a legal contract.

A further obstacle to the growth of union membership was the compilation of the **blacklist**. The blacklist was a list of workers associated in any way with unions. Employers used the list to prevent the hiring of union workers. Blacklists of workers were usually compiled by industrial spies. An undercover spy went into a work force and reported anyone who uttered a favorable remark about unions. It soon became obvious to employers that the costs of finding these "agitators" could be shared. Lists of union activists and union sympathizers were regularly sold and circulated within local, regional, and national organizations of employers.

SURVIVAL OF "PURE AND SIMPLE UNIONISM"

Before the American Federation of Labor was formed, all attempts to create a national federation of unions had failed. They fell victim to economic depressions or disastrous defeats at the polls or on the picket lines. Gompers's vision of a craft union structure focused on wages, hours, and conditions of work and avoided deep political involvement. This proved to be a form of unionism that was able to survive. Practical, "job-conscious" unionism was more compatible with the values of private enterprise, so employers and the public were less opposed to it.

Members of the Industrial Workers of the World, a radical labor union, rally in the street.

Challenge from the Left

The major rival to the AFL before World War I was a turbulent, colorful labor organization called the Industrial Workers of the World (IWW), popularly known as the Wobblies. Organized in Chicago in 1905, the IWW drew its main source of power and leadership from the Western Federation of Miners, a union that had withdrawn from the AFL in 1897.

The 1905 Chicago meeting brought together leaders of several left-wing and radical labor and political movements. These included Eugene V. Debs, founder of the American Railway Union and a Socialist Party candidate for president; Daniel DeLeon, a brilliant but eccentric socialist theoretician; and "Mother" Jones, a fiery speaker who spent 50 years organizing and agitating for the rights of coal miners.

The dominant figure at the Chicago congress, however, was the one-eyed, stoop-shouldered giant, "Big Bill" Haywood, head of the delegation from the Western Federation of Miners. Haywood had often fought the violence of company police with dynamite during the strikes that occurred as the West slowly emerged from its frontier tradition.

Under Haywood's leadership, the IWW enjoyed some short-lived but notable successes. The Wobblies' activities ranged from leading textile strikes in Massachusetts and New Jersey to organizing workers in the iron mines on Minnesota's Mesabi Range and in the logging camps and wheat fields of the Pacific Northwest. Though robust in spirit, the Wobblies did not achieve any kind of permanent organization. At peak strength, the IWW represented only about 60,000 dues-paying members.

Three important figures of the labor movement's radical left wing: Top, IWW leader William "Big Bill" Haywood; bottom left, Mary Harris Jones, known as "Mother Jones"; bottom right, Eugene V. Debs, Socialist candidate for president of the United States.

The IWW influenced the folklore and music of the labor movement
that emerged in the 1930s.

The major contributions of the IWW were keeping alive the concept of industrial unionism—the "one big union" of Haywood's vision—and influencing the folk-lore and style of the great labor movement that was to emerge in the 1930s. Much of the picket-line marching music and many of the folk ballads and militant hymns of the labor movement were written with crusading zeal by Wobbly minstrels who traveled the country's railways in boxcars, trying to build one big union.

The decline of the IWW began with its leaders arguing over theory, a problem common to left-wing movements. The organization fell apart after opposing the United States' involvement in World War I. More than 100 IWW leaders were imprisoned during the war. Others fled the country to escape prosecution under the Sedition Act of 1918, which made it a crime to publish or write anything critical of the U.S. form of government, Constitution, military or naval forces, flag, or uniform. Many Wobblies became victims of a wave of anti-Communist hysteria—the "red scare"—that swept the country following the Russian Revolution in 1917. Attorney General Mitchell Palmer deported many "Reds" and raided the offices of any suspect organizations. By the early 1920s, the IWW had ceased to exist as a functioning labor organization.

INDUSTRIAL WARFARE IN THE 20TH CENTURY

During the early years of the 20th century, the militant spirit of the IWW and the growing strength of the AFL led more employers to oppose unionism. Strikes were usually crushed with vigorous force. A report submitted to Congress in 1915 about violence against a group of striking miners and their families contained this description:

> . . . the [company] militia opened rifle and machine gun fire killing five men and one boy and firing the tents with a torch. Eleven children and two women of the colony were burnt to death. Hundreds of women and children

were driven terror-stricken into the hills while others huddled for 12 hours in pits underneath their tents while bullets from machine guns whistled overhead and kept them in constant terror.

Other reports of massacres of striking workers came from Gary, Indiana, where 18 were killed and dozens wounded. Miners suffered defeats in strikes in Idaho, Tennessee, Pennsylvania, and West Virginia.

In the great steel strike of 1919, 300,000 immigrant steelworkers drifted back to the mills after spending more than 100 futile days on the picket lines. A coalition of Protestant churches attempted to mediate the dispute but was turned away by the steel companies. The church group issued a report concluding that

> the United States Steel Corporation was too big to be beaten by 300,000 workingmen. It had too large a cash surplus, too many allies among other businesses, too much support from government officers, local and national, too strong influence with the press—it spread over too much of the earth—still retaining absolutely centralized control, to be defeated by widely scattered workers of many minds, many fears, varying states of pocketbook, and under a comparatively improvised leadership.

The collapse of unionism in the basic industries following the steel strike was to last another 15 years.

Labor in the 1920s

The 1920s was a decade of unprecedented industrial growth. Between 1922 and 1929, the output of agriculture, manufacturing, mining, and construction increased 34 percent.

Workers inspect automobiles coming down an early assembly line at the Ford Motor Company. The growing automobile industry contributed to the country's economic prosperity during the 1920s.

Fed by the new automobile, radio, and farm equipment industries, and sustained by highway and real estate development, the economy rolled forward at a brisk pace. Only a handful of bankers and university economists were sounding a warning. They saw several signs of serious trouble ahead for the economy. **Stocks** were selling for more than they were worth. Farm prices were down. The economists were dismissed as alarmists, but their predictions were soon fulfilled. The seven fat years of 1922–1929 were followed by the seven leanest years that the U.S. economy had ever experienced.

During the seven prosperous years, the labor movement had fallen to a low-water mark. The labor movement struggled to survive during the prosperous "Roaring Twenties" and was reborn during the Great Depression of the 1930s. It reached its peak during World War II.

Union membership fell sharply during the 1920s, mainly because employers began using a set of strategies which historians have labeled "welfare capitalism." The main features of welfare capitalism were:

- *The American Plan:* Some employer associations worked to establish the **open shop** system. Under this system, employers refused to recognize a union in hiring procedures. Even the **union shop**, which gave the employer a free hand in hiring workers but required union membership thereafter, was strongly opposed.
- *Company representation plans:* The open-shop drive was reinforced by employee organizations that were dominated by company employers and did not fairly represent the interests of workers.
- *Company benefit programs:* Fringe benefit programs were installed by many corporations. The programs often included such features as stock distribution and profit-sharing plans, social clubs, sports programs, health clinics, low-rent housing, and even recreational parks built close to the plants.
- *Scientific management:* Scientific management emphasized efficiency through job study, improvements in methods, and work incentives. It helped productivity to grow rapidly during the 1920s.

Throughout the decade, employers continued to use the blacklist, the yellow-dog contract, and the injunction. Union membership slipped from 5 million in 1920 to 3.5 million in 1923.

Welfare capitalism sapped the strength of the labor movement at a time when the AFL also faced a change in leadership. In 1924 Samuel Gompers died. He was succeeded by the mild-mannered William Green, head of the United Mine Workers. Green could not match Gompers's vigorous leadership of the AFL.

In spite of the decline of the labor movement during this decade, one positive accomplishment stands out. Sam Gompers's AFL, built on the principle of "pure and simple unionism," survived attacks by hostile courts and welfare capitalism.

The economic prosperity of the 1920s—created by a combination of new products, new ideas, and efficient production methods—was accompanied by an era of labor-management harmony. It seemed that this harmony might continue permanently. The stock market crash of 1929 signaled an end to this feeling of confidence and a harsh return to reality.

The Great Depression

In October 1929, the New York Stock Exchange was shaken by a slide in stock prices, which grew more threatening by the hour. On October 24, the slide worsened. A group of investors tried to stem the growing panic. For a short time, the **stock market** seemed to recover, but on October 29, it fell apart. Frantic sellers sold 16 million shares of stock.

The economic structure of the United States collapsed— the bottom fell out of the stock market. Businesses were suddenly worthless; people who owned shares, or parts, of those businesses saw their money disappear. People who had invested money in the market were left with nothing, or very little. Thirty billion dollars' worth of investments had vanished. The decade following the stock market crash is known as the Great Depression.

It was a time of contradiction, confusion, rootlessness, and fear. Warehouses were bursting with unsold goods while breadlines were forming in the streets of major cities. By 1933 about 14 million U.S. workers—nearly one out of every three—were unemployed. Millions lost their homes and farms, and clusters of shacks, called "Hoovervilles," sprang up across the country.

The tragedy deepened as a severe drought hit the heartlands of the Midwest and south central states. For several years, little or no rain fell on the croplands. Then the wind began to pick up the powder-dry soil, resulting in furious dust storms that blackened the skies for days, burying the already scorched crops. The meager crops, often unsellable because few people had money to buy them, brought little cash income.

Refugees from the great "dust bowls" were forced from their lands. Banks, which were also shaken by the crisis, seized farms as payment from farmers who owed the banks money. Armies of farm families, called "Okies" (from Oklahoma) regardless of point of origin, loaded their cars and farm trucks and fanned out to the West looking for work. There was little to be found. When work was available, there were always more job seekers than jobs. As a result, wages were pitifully low.

In 1933 hope was renewed in the nation by the confident message of the new president, Franklin Delano Roosevelt. He spoke of "one-third of a nation ill-fed, ill-housed and ill-clothed," but he insisted that "the only thing we have to fear is fear itself."

The Roosevelt administration initiated a flood of legislation which came to be known as "The New Deal."

A farmer and his two children run for cover during a dust storm. Severe drought in the 1930s created the "dust bowl" in the Midwest and south central states.

The New Deal permanently altered the role of government in the economy. Some measures the government took included: insuring bank deposits with federal money, so that people would not lose money if the bank failed; requiring more detailed information be given to the public about stocks sold on the market; and providing jobs for the jobless.

During the Depression, Congress passed a series of pro-labor laws to encourage the practice of collective bargaining. The Norris-LaGuardia Act of 1932 forbade the use of yellow-dog contracts and limited the use of injunctions in labor disputes. This legislation was followed by Section 7A of the National Industrial Recovery Act (NIRA), which provided that employees should have the right to form unions of their own choosing, free from employer control or direction.

Most of the NIRA was later ruled unconstitutional, but Section 7A was incorporated into the major labor law of the century. This law was the National Labor Relations Act of 1935, usually called the Wagner Act after its sponsor, Senator Robert Wagner of New York. The Wagner Act guaranteed the right of workers to organize and to bargain collectively with their employers. It also made company unions illegal. The act created the National Labor Relations Board, an agency that would determine if a majority of workers genuinely wanted to be represented by a particular union. The Board would also enforce the legislative requirement that bargaining be carried on in good faith. The passage of the Wagner Act signaled the rebirth of the labor movement.

The CIO and the Drive to Organize

At the 1935 AFL convention, two men of similar backgrounds but dramatically different temperaments debated a central issue of trade union philosophy, craft versus industrial unionism. William Green, presiding over the convention, and John L. Lewis, then president of the United Mine Workers, were both sons of immigrant Welsh miners. Both had risen to power through the United Mine Workers, the AFL's largest union. There the similarity ended.

Green was a mild and unimaginative man who had pledged upon his election to the AFL presidency "to adhere to those fundamental purposes of trade unionism so amply championed by Gompers." John L. Lewis, by contrast, was a dramatic man of heroic proportions. Over six feet tall, with a huge mane of black hair and bushy

The fiery John L. Lewis split off from the AFL to lead the Committee for Industrial Organization, which later became the Congress of Industrial Organizations (CIO).

brows, he had a deep, resonant voice and a startling command of language. Born in a coal-mining region near Lucas, Iowa, Lewis was renowned for his tremendous physical strength and fierce courage.

Lewis, a proponent of industrial unions, argued for the inclusion in a single union of all levels and kinds of workers: skilled and unskilled, recent immigrants, women, and blacks. This was the only kind of organization, he claimed, that could generate enough strength to successfully unionize the basic, mass-production industries.

Green disagreed entirely. As he saw it, the experience of labor in the 1920s had demonstrated that a federation of unions of skilled workers separated into crafts—carpenters, bricklayers, electricians, and so forth—was the only structure that could survive permanently.

The debate was furious. Lewis seemed to revel in the fight. "They are striking at me hip and thigh," he reported, "right merrily shall I return their blows." Finally the AFL leadership agreed to the establishment of a Committee for Industrial Organization.

The truce was temporary, however. Following a fist-fight with an AFL member, John L. Lewis resigned as vice-president of the AFL. He then led the Committee for Industrial Organization in an energetic organizing drive in the basic industries—steel, auto, textile, rubber, chemical, and many others. In 1937 the 10 unions that made up the committee were expelled from the AFL. The committee was renamed the Congress of Industrial Organizations (CIO) in 1938. The split between the two great federations was to last for almost 20 years.

The craft versus industrial union fight that led to the formation of the CIO could not be resolved by the decisions of the union leaders alone. The real issues of the struggle surfaced on the picket lines of Akron and Pittsburgh, in the sit-down strikes of Flint and Cleveland, in the pitched battles on the streets of Minneapolis and Chicago. The giant corporations were not about to passively accept the unionization of their enterprises.

As Steel Goes, So Goes the Nation

Basic industries such as steel manufacturing fought

attempts to unionize for years. In the 1930s, one Pennsylvania steel company staged fake "hearings" of union activists. A local judge, with the help of the county jail doctor and an attorney who served as a deputy for the steel company, judged the union activists to be insane and committed them to a mental institution. When this was discovered, the governor of the state had the activists released from custody.

The resistance of Republic Steel Corporation, while more open, proved no less stubborn. On Memorial Day 1937, over 100 striking steelworkers at Republic's Chicago plant were shot at. Ten men were killed, 67 arrested; no weapons were found among the strikers. Republic Steel had been well prepared to defend its plants against the striking workers. A committee investigating the outbreak of industrial warfare found that the company had spent $43,901 in two months for armaments, including 92 riot guns, 2,295 long-range projectiles, 326 short-range gas cartridges, 2,029 gas grenades, and tear and sickening gas.

In response to the use of armies of paid strikebreakers backed by police and militia, strikers organized **sit-down strikes**. In a sit-down strike, employees refuse to work or to leave the plant. They "sit down" on the job. This kind of strike was rarely used before 1935.

The first major sit-down strike of the 1930s occurred at the Hormel Packing Company in Austin, Minnesota, where 2,500 workers sat in the plant for three days in 1933. They won an increase in wages and a reduction in their work load. The sit-down strike came into widespread use after another effective sit-down strike by rubber workers in Akron, Ohio, in 1935. The technique

Police opened fire on striking steelworkers at the Republic Steel Corporation on Memorial Day, 1937.

was perfected by striking autoworkers, who at one point closed plants employing 140,000 General Motors workers.

Following a 44-day sit-in in 1937, the autoworkers' union was **exclusively recognized** by General Motors as the sole bargaining representative for the employees.

After this breakthrough and the recognition of the steel-workers union by the head of the giant U.S. Steel Corporation, the campaign to organize the basic industries moved forward briskly. By 1940 the number of union members had grown from less than 3 million in 1933 to over 9 million. At the end of World War II, 18.5 million workers were members of AFL and CIO unions.

Labor with a capital "L" now represented the largest single organized sector of U.S. society. More than one out of every three non-farm workers were covered by a labor agreement. At last the widespread violence and bloodshed that had disrupted labor-management relations for nearly a century came to an end. The modern era of industrial relations was born.

Workers at General Motors participated in a sit-down strike for 44 days in 1937. Their efforts won them union representation.

ORGANIZED LABOR IN WORLD WAR II

When the United States declared war against Japan and Germany in 1941, President Roosevelt secured a no-strike pledge from the AFL, the CIO, and the railroad unions. Despite giving up the right to strike during World War II, the labor movement grew at a rate of nearly a million workers a year between 1941 and 1945. In order to meet the huge production goals for war materials, employers relaxed their opposition to unionism, and membership reached an all-time high.

Thousands of committees with members from both labor and

management worked to improve efficiency. Labor disputes declined to near zero. The National War Labor Board, created by the government to settle wartime labor disputes, proved effective in resolving disagreements.

The need for workers in war industries also paved the way for thousands of women and minority workers to gain jobs in industries formerly closed to them. Labor shortages caused by the departure of millions of workers into the armed services opened up even more job opportunities.

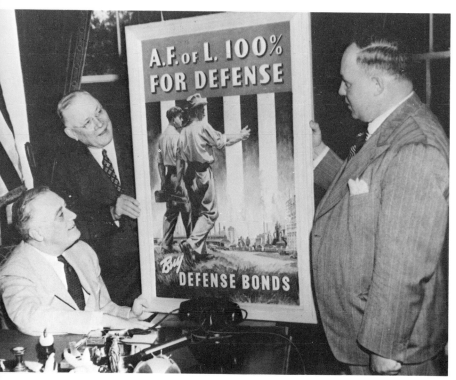

Labor leaders William Green (second from left) and George Meany (right) show an American Federation of Labor defense poster to President Franklin Delano Roosevelt.

During World War II, posters of "Rosie the Riveter" urged women to work in factories. More than six million women entered the work force during the war. It was the first opportunity for many of them to work outside the home.

The war years also saw the emergence of a new wave of union leadership. John L. Lewis's influence declined sharply after he opposed a third term for President Franklin D. Roosevelt. Roosevelt was an extremely popular president, especially among labor unions. Most workers rebuffed Lewis's endorsement of presidential candidate Wendell Wilkie, and Lewis handed over the reins of the CIO to Philip Murray.

Murray soon established himself as a great labor leader. On the issue of wartime labor policy, Phil Murray supported the no-strike pledge and cooperation with the War Labor Board.

LABOR IN THE POSTWAR PERIOD

After the war, people all over the United States were becoming alarmed about Communist influence in the world. Within the CIO, some members expressed fears about Communist influence in certain CIO unions. Fearing that the CIO could not survive the internal struggles over this and other issues, Philip Murray chose to do battle with the left-wing radicals. In a series of administrative hearings, the CIO expelled 11 unions on the grounds of "dual unionism"—a term that meant that these unions were being used by their leaders to further the interests of Communism.

9

A Scottish immigrant, Philip Murray served as president of the United Steelworkers of America and the CIO during the 1940s.

Many labor historians question the wisdom of the CIO expulsion. It cost the labor organization almost one-third of its membership. It lost some of its best leaders, most of whom were not Communists, but simply had unpopular opinions about foreign policy. After the expulsion, the CIO became increasingly conservative.

The economic and political climate of the United States shifted dramatically after World War II. During the war, labor-management conflicts had been muted by the pressing need for cooperation in the war effort. The end of the war brought changes which were to affect the labor movement profoundly for the next generation.

Employers faced difficult problems. They had to absorb millions of returning GIs (U.S. soldiers) into industries. At the same time, they had to make the complex transition from producing war materials to making consumer goods. Most economists were predicting that this change would cause serious problems. Many experts forecast a major recession.

During the war, the government had controlled wage levels. Workers also worked overtime, increasing their wages. After the war, workers could not count on earning extra money by working overtime, and they hoped to make up for that lost overtime income. Employers and workers with disputes no longer had to yield to decisions of the War Labor Board. As a result, labor-management relationships broke down. Many negotiators discovered that their bargaining skills had eroded after years of letting the Board settle differences. The results were not surprising—1946 was a record year for strikes.

While the strikes were not violent, as they had been in previous years, more people were affected in 1946. During the years 1935–39, an average of 19 million person-days per year were lost to strikes. In 1946 this figure rocketed to 116 million. There were major strikes in the steel, coal, and automobile industries, on the railroads, and in shipping and air transport.

The Taft-Hartley Act

Public attitudes toward unions shifted in response to the 1946 outbreak of strikes. Weary of war and conflict, the nation was becoming more conservative. Congress responded to industrial unrest and the apparent change in public opinion by passing the Taft-Hartley Act in 1947.

President Harry S Truman vetoed the Taft-Hartley Act, characterizing it as "shocking, bad for labor, bad for management, bad for the country." Congress passed the bill over the president's veto.

The Taft-Hartley Act was essentially a series of major amendments to the Wagner Act of 1935. The act was intended to adjust the balance of government intervention in labor-management affairs. The Wagner Act had set the basic labor policy of the federal government: to actively encourage the growth of collective bargaining. The act allowed workers to organize unions of their own choosing, without employer interference. The act also made it illegal for employers to dominate what happened within a union and required employers to "bargain in good faith with duly certified unions."

The Taft-Hartley Act attempted to extend a series of corollary, or parallel, rights to management. Unions were now also required to bargain in good faith. Employers were permitted to sue for damages for breach of contract. Strikes could not be called without 60 days' notice if a valid contract was in effect. The **closed shop**, in which only union members could be hired, was outlawed.

Other provisions, however, appeared to go beyond the limits of "corollary rights." These provisions angered labor leaders. For example, union leaders were required to file sworn statements that they were not Communists. No such requirement was forced on employers. Trade unionists attacked this provision as discriminatory. Some prominent leaders, including John L. Lewis, a noted anti-Communist, refused to file the statement. This feature of the law was later repealed.

Another provision of the Taft-Hartley Act that labor firmly opposed was Section 14(b), which allowed individual states to pass strict laws against unions. In the next few years, 20 states, most of them in the agricultural regions of the Midwest and in the newly industrialized

Southeast, passed so-called **right-to-work laws.** These laws prevent many union practices, such as the union shop, **maintenance-of-membership agreements**, and in some instances, the **checkoff of union dues**.

The most lasting impact of Section 14(b) is that unions in "right-to-work" states must represent _all_ workers in a bargaining unit for contract negotiations and grievances— even those workers who do not pay union dues.

Labor in the 1950s: The Impact of Modern Technology

On the heels of the Taft-Hartley Act came a series of developments which were to have even greater consequences for the labor movement. Mid-century was a time of great technological change in the U.S. Mechanization, automation, and computerization had a dramatic impact on the nation's work force. By 1956, for the first time in the history of any industrial nation, the number of **white-collar workers** in the labor force exceeded the number of **blue-collar workers**, 25.6 million to 25.2 million. The effects of the new technology were felt most keenly in the basic industries—manufacturing, mining, and transportation, traditional strongholds of trade union power.

New jobs were being created primarily in areas such as services and trades, the professions, finance, insurance, and state and local governments—all areas of employment that were not highly unionized. The result was a long-term decline in union membership. Union membership fell from almost 37 percent of the nonfarm labor force in 1945 to 28 percent in 1969.

George Meany (left) and Walter Reuther (right) exuberantly announce the formation of the AFL-CIO in 1955.

Dramatic losses in union membership occurred in the basic industries, while the teamsters, retail clerks, teachers, and state, county, and municipal workers unions were all counting substantial membership gains. Gains in these areas almost equaled losses in industrial unions.

Faced with new technology and the loss of political favor, the two major labor federations moved to close the gap that had divided the labor movement for 20 years. The new technology blurred the distinctions between skilled craftspeople and factory production-line workers. Most unions had been forced to adopt a structure that included both kinds of workers. The arguments that had caused the rift between the AFL and CIO in 1937 were no longer so important.

On November 9, 1952, Philip Murray, president of the CIO, died of a heart attack. Just 12 days later, his counterpart in the AFL, William Green, also died. The work of reconciliation went forward, and on February 9, 1955, a merger agreement was announced by the new presidents of the rival federations. Walter Reuther of the CIO and George Meany of the AFL signed the merger agreement to create the new AFL-CIO.

The Rise and Fall of Labor Racketeering in the U.S.

The merger of the AFL and the CIO spelled the beginning of the end of racketeering as a significant factor in organized labor. Racketeering means making money from an illegal activity. The influence of racketeers in some AFL unions dates back to the Prohibition era.

During the 1950s, the influence of racketeers in the labor movement dwindled. Racketeering in labor unions began during the Prohibition era, back in the 1920s. Above, illegal alcohol is discovered hidden in a truckful of lumber during Prohibition.

Congress passed the National Prohibition Act in 1919. Commonly known as the Volstead Act, the law was the 18th Amendment to the Constitution.

The Volstead Act severely restricted the manufacture and distribution of alcohol. While the law was regarded by its supporters as a boon to society, critics contend that the 14 years of Prohibition represent the most corrupt period in the nation's history. Almost from the day the law was enacted, illegal breweries and distilleries sprang up all over the country. The illegal alcoholic beverages sold to night spots known as "speakeasies" also included foreign-made liquor smuggled across the border and into seaport cities.

These widespread violations of the law spawned a new breed of racketeers called "bootleggers." They quickly worked their way into legitimate restaurant, trucking, distilling, pharmaceutical, and bakery industries. Pharmacies and bakeries became major targets for the bootleggers, because such businesses gave bootleggers a reason to buy the ingredients needed to make liquor and beer: sugar, grain products, malt, and distilled alcohol.

Gangsters also infiltrated the unions of industries associated with the making, transporting, or selling of liquor. Racketeers used both bribes and violence to get into legitimate businesses and unions. Some historians estimate that more than 500 business and union leaders were killed by gangsters during this period. About 1,300 gangsters and peace officers were killed in enforcement raids. Estimates of the number of people slain in warfare between rival gangs of racketeers number in the several thousands.

Unfortunately, racketeering in U.S. business and unions did not disappear with the repeal of Prohibition in 1933. These corrupt groups found new illegal activities to exploit. Labor racketeers stole union funds and demanded money from employers in return for peace with the unions. Sometimes corrupt businesspeople conspired with equally corrupt union leaders to force lower wages on workers through so-called sweetheart contracts.

Eventually, reform movements within unions and effective federal prosecution of union racketeers succeeded in eliminating racketeering from the labor movement. Corruption can still be found in the labor movement, just as in business, government, and religious organizations. For the most part, however, labor racketeering was eradicated by the mid-1960s.

HIGH-WATER MARK AND THE RECEDING TIDE

The founding convention of the merged AFL-CIO struck a theme of exuberant enthusiasm. President George Meany promised the delegates that the movement would use "every legal means . . . to organize the unorganized" and vowed that "no little men with loud voices in either political or industrial life are going to turn us aside." Indeed, the first decade following the 1955 merger saw substantial economic and political gains under the banner of the new federation.

During the 1960s, the majority of U.S. workers were employed in white-collar jobs such as banking.

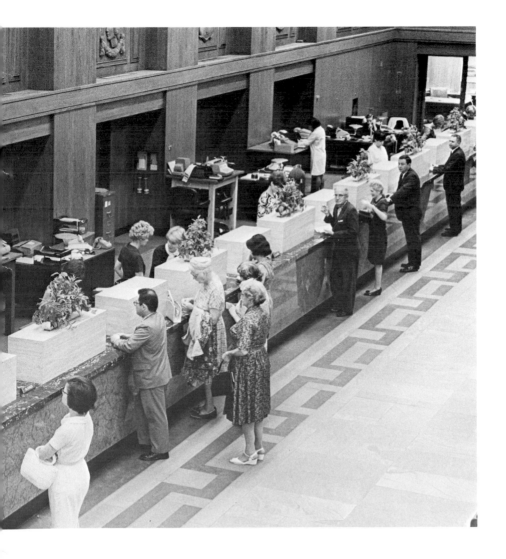

10

Among the successes was the rapid growth of pension (retirement) programs for working people, a benefit few workers enjoyed before the 1950s. By 1965 pensions were a common feature of most labor contracts, as were health insurance programs and cost-of-living adjustment (COLA) provisions, which allow workers' salaries to rise as the cost of living goes up. Wages also continued to climb.

On the political front, the AFL-CIO fulfilled another aspect of George Meany's goal of making "our full contribution to the welfare of our neighbors . . . and to the nation as a whole." Organized labor was in the thick of the battle to pass the civil rights acts of the mid-1960s. The AFL-CIO gave high legislative priority to consumer protection, improvements in social security, raising the minimum wage, and other laws that would benefit the community at large as well as union membership. By pursuing political and social concerns, organized labor hoped to serve as "the people's lobby"—the people's representative in the government.

Despite these successes, warning signs began to surface, pointing to a difficult period ahead for the labor movement. As the nation entered the 1970s, union membership began to slip rapidly, making it clear that organized labor had passed its post-World War II high-water mark and was caught in a receding tide.

The Passing of the Old Guard

In 1970 the labor movement was shaken by the death of Walter Reuther, the dynamic leader of the United Auto Workers (UAW) and head of the CIO at the time

Under the dynamic leadership of Walter Reuther, the United Auto Workers pioneered many new benefits for U.S. workers.

of its merger with the AFL. Reuther died in an airplane crash on his way to celebrate the opening of the UAW Family and Education Center at Black Lake, Michigan. Reuther had won the presidency of the UAW in a bitter campaign against that union's radical left wing. He went on to earn worldwide respect for his innovative ideas in collective bargaining. Under his leadership, the UAW pioneered many new worker benefit programs.

Reuther's partner in the formation of the AFL-CIO, George Meany, retired as president of the AFL-CIO in 1979. He died one year later. Widely respected as a man of great courage and honesty, Meany guided the federation with a firm hand through its formative years.

George Meany's successor as president of the AFL-CIO, Lane Kirkland, brings a new dimension of leadership to the federation. Kirkland is often referred to by the press as a "labor statesman." He assumed leadership of the AFL-CIO at a time when the winds of political and economic change shifted sharply to organized labor's disadvantage.

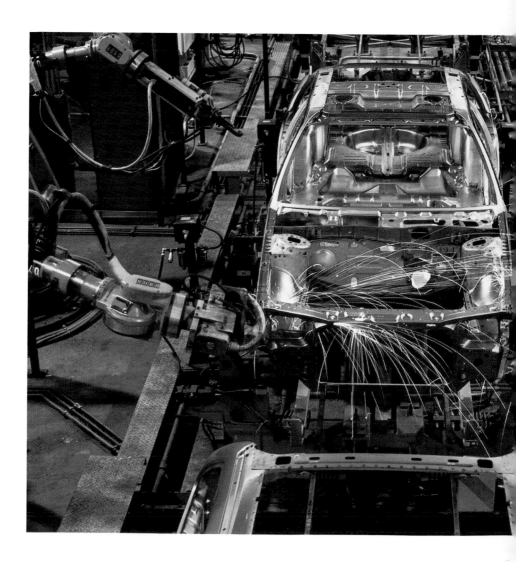

11

CHANGING TIMES, CHANGING DIRECTIONS

The 1970s and '80s brought continuing changes in technology and international trade. Advanced automation—including the increased use of robots—reduced the number of jobs available in the nation's basic industries—manufacturing, mining, transportation, and agriculture.

Although U.S. industry remained productive, its position as a leader in the international marketplace had been eroding since the 1950s. Industrial nations in Europe and Asia saw robust development in their basic industries during the 1970s and '80s. Because these nations did not

Gas shortages in the 1970s resulted in long lines at service stations. The energy crisis prompted the U.S. auto industry to begin manufacturing more fuel-efficient cars.

have heavy defense budgets like the United States, they were able to spend large amounts of money building their economies.

Foreign companies in turn invested in European and Asian industries. The nations of Asia and Europe continue to outpace the United States in many important areas of technological development.

A further blow hit the U.S. economy in the 1970s when the Oil Producing and Exporting Communities (OPEC) sharply cut production. Energy costs soared. At the time, U.S. automobile companies were still producing big, "gas-guzzling" cars. Soon long lines were forming at filling stations, where gasoline was scarce and costly.

It took several years for the automobile industry to

design more fuel-efficient cars. By then, many U.S. consumers had bought foreign-made cars and trucks. By the mid-1980s, about two out of every five cars on U.S. roads were produced abroad.

The United States lost its competitive advantage not only in the automobile industry, but in almost every major sector of manufacturing. A quick check of clothing labels in any department store shows the loss of American jobs in the textile and apparel industries. A visit to an electronics store reveals how Japan dominates this market.

Increased competition from industrial nations as well as from the developing or "Third World" countries led to a change in the kinds of jobs being created in the U.S. Fewer jobs were available in the highly unionized basic industries, while employment grew in the less organized service and trades industries, such as fast-food restaurants, retail shops, data processing firms, banking, and insurance.

At the same time, manufacturing companies moved from the highly unionized Northeast and Midwest to the "Sunbelt" region of the South, where the political and social climate was less receptive to unions. Public officials in the Sunbelt states have attracted industries from the more unionized northern states by offering tax concessions, lower unemployment and workers' compensation benefits, and state legislation that is hostile to union-organizing activities, such as right-to-work laws.

These changes in the location and composition of jobs resulted in a steady decline in union membership as a percentage of the labor force. By 1982 total union membership reached a low of 19.8 million, almost 1 million

By the 1980s, the United States was no longer the leader in the international marketplace. Japanese automobiles and electronics were among the foreign products selling well in the U.S. As a result of foreign competition and other changes in U.S. manufacturing, fewer jobs are available in the nation's highly unionized basic industries.

fewer members than in 1968. More significantly, between 1970 and 1989, union membership fell from 25.7 to 16.8 percent of the total work force.

One reason it has been difficult to organize employees in service and professional occupations is that people in these kinds of jobs tend to be highly mobile. They change employers more frequently and move into higher-paid positions more rapidly. Consequently, service and professional employees tend to expect that their financial success depends more on their own efforts and talents than on a general improvement in compensation for the whole work force.

Further, service employees change jobs rather rapidly. Union organizing is usually more successful in larger, more stable work forces, where an employee is more likely to rely on improvements in wages and working conditions for all employees to provide economic advancement for the individual.

During the 1970s and '80s, the number of jobs available in services, such as fast-food restaurants, grew faster than the number of jobs available in the basic industries.

In recent years, many employers have hired professional consultants who devise programs to avoid unionization of a company. These consultants, usually psychologists and lawyers, convince employees that they do not need a labor union to achieve decent wages and fair treatment from the employers. For example, the employer will match the wage paid in the unionized sector of the same industry. Two-way communications programs are also set up to deal with employee problems before workers turn to a labor union for help. In many ways, union avoidance programs are a tribute to the past successes of organized labor. These programs promise workers the fruits of unionism without workers having to pay union dues.

In recent years, the National Labor Relations Board has moved away from its historical role of encouraging collective bargaining as a means of promoting industrial peace. The emerging policy of the NLRB is to serve as a neutral referee between employers and unions. While employers generally applaud the new direction in NLRB policy, labor leaders contend that, far from being neutral, the Board now favors employers.

Union membership fell in the 1980s to its lowest point since the early years of the Great Depression. Those who predict the demise of the labor movement, however, would do well to remember what Mark Twain said when he learned that a newspaper had published his obituary: "Reports of my death have been greatly exaggerated."

Looking to the Future

Perhaps the greatest value to the student of history is

the development of perspective—the long view, which saves us from jumping to premature conclusions on the basis of recent events. The long view of history tells us that the labor movement, with roots dating to the origins of this nation, has survived many crises, only to emerge stronger than in the past.

Despite the bleak period of the past 15 years, the labor movement has scored many solid successes. Impressive gains in organizing and representing public-sector employees have been registered. A generation ago only the uniformed public employees—firefighters, postal workers, police officers—were substantially unionized. By 1989 most public school teachers were represented by collective bargaining organizations, and nearly 40 percent of all other federal, state, county, and municipal employees were organized. Other areas in which unions have made solid organizing gains include the health-care industry and professional sports.

Unions of professional entertainers have long represented musicians and actors, as well as radio and television announcers. In recent years, these unions have successfully extended their membership to include symphony orchestras, opera and ballet companies, and studio engineers and technicians in the electronic media.

And yet, these gains in white-collar, professional, technical, and entertainment fields have not compensated for the far greater loss of union membership in manufacturing, mining, and transportation. The evidence shows, however, that unions have gained momentum in areas previously resistant to effective organization. As unionism grows in these occupations, it is reasonable to expect an eventual resurgence in total union membership.

Union membership has declined in the basic industries, such as construction, manufacturing, mining, and transportation.

In some areas of employment, however, union membership has increased. Orchestra members (above) and other entertainment industry employees have unions, as do public sector employees like teachers (below) and police.

An important aspect of the changing labor movement will be the emergence of new union leadership. As more professional and technical occupations become unionized, we can expect to see their interests represented more thoroughly and these sectors contribute to the top ranks of union leadership.

The new generation of union leaders is finding creative approaches to meet the challenges facing organized labor in the decades ahead. AFL-CIO president Lane Kirkland has responded to the problems of declining union membership and reverses on the political front by launching new programs in the areas of organizing, public relations, educating union leadership, and building political coalitions with women's and minority groups. Kirkland recently formed the AFL-CIO Labor Institute of Public Affairs to help communicate labor's point of view on social and economic issues.

In 1982 the AFL-CIO established a Committee on the Evolution of Work. The committee evaluated organized labor's response to the wide-ranging changes taking place in the U.S. labor force. Its initial report, *The Future of Work,* predicts the impact of new technology on the kinds of jobs Americans will perform in the decades ahead. The report suggests changes unions must make in organizing strategies and collective bargaining agendas to better represent new workers entering the labor force.

In 1985 the Committee on the Evolution of Work completed a second and even more sweeping analysis of the problems facing American workers. The 1985 report, entitled *The Changing Situation of Workers and Their Unions,* discussed the fast pace of change in the nature of work, the organization of the workplace, and the composition of the labor force. These changes explain the declining income of younger workers. As the economy shifts from its historical emphasis on manufacturing, construction, farming, and mining to a service-oriented work force, wage rates are going down. Low-paid unskilled jobs in fast-food outlets and retail stores are replacing high-paid skilled jobs in the basic industries.

The report projected that in 1990, service industries will employ three out of every four workers in the U.S. Only 10 percent of service industry employees are unionized, however. Unlike the long-term, well-paid jobs in the basic industries, the lower-paid service jobs tend to be unstable and employ many part-time workers.

The Committee's analysis of the nation's labor laws and the conservative shift of the National Labor Relations Board shows that organized labor no longer can count on government neutrality in labor-management relationships. Recent NLRB rulings have limited workers' ability to organize into unions of their own choosing. Employers have demonstrated increasing hostility to union-organizing attempts.

The Changing Situation of Workers and Their Unions concludes with a call to action:

> . . . the labor movement cannot be content with defending the status quo, or reliving past glories. We must constantly look to the future, develop new leadership, adapt policies to changing conditions and new technologies, but—always, always—with unswerving loyalty to the mission of the trade union movement as the instrument for improving and enhancing the working and living conditions of those who work for wages.

> *President George Meany at 1979 Convention*

12

CONTRIBUTIONS OF UNIONS TO AMERICAN LIFE

No history of the labor movement in the United States can overlook the contributions that workers' unions have made to American society. The obvious fruits of collective bargaining include decent wages, safer workplaces, pensions to provide income security in retirement, freedom from unfair treatment on the job, recourse from unjust firing, as well as paid holidays and vacations.

Not so easily seen are the many contributions organized labor has made to progressive legislation which has benefitted all Americans. The father of public education, Horace Mann, wrote that the labor movement stood as his staunchest ally in the fight for free schools as the right of every child. Organized labor led the struggle for the eight-hour workday at a time when workers toiled from sunrise to sunset. Children would probably still work in some industries had it not been for the labor movement's crusade to pass the nation's child labor laws—a victory that was not fully achieved until as late as 1949.

Long before the passage of the Civil Rights Act of 1964, most labor contracts prohibited discrimination in employment on the basis of race, gender, age, or religious belief. When Martin Luther King, Jr., led his famous March on Washington to press for civil rights legislation, he strode to the Lincoln Memorial arm in arm with labor leader Walter Reuther. The AFL-CIO headquarters in Washington, D.C., provided Dr. King's staff with office space and financial support for that famous march, which opened the doors of opportunity for millions of citizens.

The late George Meany referred to the labor movement as "the people's lobby." Meany's phrase continues to be a valid claim under his successor, AFL-CIO president Lane Kirkland. In 1989 organized labor fought for laws that would improve health care, support public education, meet the needs of working women, offer tax support for low- and moderate-priced housing, and generate job opportunities for the unemployed.

Other issues that concern organized labor include: protection of employees' privacy and dignity; opposition to required drug testing; and protection against sexual harassment and sexual discrimination in the workplace.

Lane Kirkland (left) and George Meany (center) at the 1979 AFL-CIO convention. That year Kirkland took over as AFL-CIO president.

The standards set in labor contracts often establish ground rules even for nonunion employees. Employers trying to avoid unionization of their work force commonly adopt the terms and conditions of employment used in labor contracts in order to persuade workers that they do not need to pay union dues to enjoy union benefits. Thus, labor movement successes improve wages and working conditions for all workers.

Organized labor has faced difficult times over the past 25 years. Even so, the historical record shows that the labor movement must be recognized as not only a major but a permanent institution. As the labor movement approaches the 21st century, the complex economic and social problems that cloud the future of the U.S. make even more vital the need for a strong voice to speak for American workers.

GLOSSARY

apprentice—one who is bound to serve a master craftsman for a specified amount of time to learn a skill or trade

arbitration—the final and binding settlement of a labor dispute by a neutral third party selected by the employer and the union, who agree to abide by the arbitrator's decision

blacklist—a means of defeating union-organizing campaigns by circulating among employers the names of workers known to favor unions or who had been active in union affairs in the past. Now illegal.

blue-collar workers—those who perform manual work, such as factory workers, truck drivers, construction workers, firefighters, and highway crews—as compared with **white-collar workers** such as teachers, nurses, flight attendants, musicians, and retail clerks

boycott—the refusal to use or buy the goods or services of an employer involved in a labor dispute, in order to bring economic pressure on the employer to settle the dispute on terms favorable to the union

checkoff of union dues—a system under which the employer agrees to deduct union dues from employees' paychecks and to put the dues directly into the union treasury

closed shop—a company where, by agreement with the union, only union members may be employed

collective action—includes all forms of concerted activities, such as boycotts, picket signs, and political organizing, by workers in labor disputes

collective bargaining—negotiations between unions and employers toward agreement on wages, terms, and conditions of employment

cottage industries—small manufacturing or processing businesses operated in the home of the business owner

craft union—a union that represents primarily skilled workers in a particular trade or craft, such as carpenters, plumbers, electricians, and printers

exclusive recognition—giving a particular union the right to serve as the sole bargaining representative for an identified group of workers who make up the "bargaining unit"

free worker—one who completed indentured status or was released from slavery by the slave owner

guild—early form of trade association

indentured service—a contracted commitment to remain in the employ of a master for a stated number of years for low and sometimes no wages

industrial homework—work performed at home on a price-per-piece basis

industrial union—a union that represents all workers, regardless of skill level, who are employed in a particular industry or location; steelworkers, autoworkers, and clothing workers belong to industrial unions

injunction—a written order of a court prohibiting a certain act. Until Congress limited the use of the injunction in labor disputes in 1932, these court orders were commonly issued in employers' behalf to prevent unions from striking or picketing

journeyman—an independent worker who has learned a skill or trade

maintenance-of-membership agreement—a provision in a labor contract requiring a worker to remain a union member as long as the contract is in effect

master craftsman—a worker who has his own shop and is qualified to teach apprentices

open shop—a company that has no form of union security agreement with the bargaining representative

picket line—a moving group of strikers who usually carry signs stating the union's position in a labor dispute

right of free association—the constitutional guarantee of the right to organize groups of people around a common concern

right-to-work laws—laws existing in some states that forbid agreements between unions and employers requiring that employees be union members to be hired or to keep a job

sit-down strike—an illegal form of strike in which the workers refuse to work or to leave the employer's premises

stock—a small part of ownership in a company. A corporation's stock is usually divided into shares. The stock owners are called stockholders or shareholders

stock market—the market in which shares of stock in companies are bought and sold

strike—the concerted withdrawal of labor services from the workplace

strikebreakers—people paid to displace employees who are on strike

white-collar workers—See **blue-collar workers**.

union shop—a form of union security agreement in which the employer does not have to hire union members but requires new employees to become union members within a certain period after being hired

yellow-dog contract—an agreement signed by a worker not to join a union while employed by the company. The Norris-LaGuardia Act of 1932 outlawed the yellow-dog contract, so named as a term of derision for any worker willing to take a job under such a condition of hire

INDEX

King, Martin Luther, Jr., 104
Kirkland, Lane, 89, 100, 104, 105
Knights of Labor, 47, 48

labor unions: employers' opposition to, 49-51, 58-60, 62, 63, 68-70, 73, 96, 105; federations of, 44, 47, 49, 52, 54; laws affecting, 40-43, 65-66, 79-81; membership in, 62, 73, 81-83, 88, 93-94, 96, 97, 98-99; organizing efforts by, 31, 40-44, 47, 49, 51, 66-69, 94, 97, 100, 101; origins of, 8-15; radical and left-wing, 53, 54-57; political activities of, 43-45, 88, 100, 104; public attitudes towards, 79
Lewis, John L., 66-67, 68, 75, 80
Long Strike, 46

Meany, George, 74, 82, 83, 86, 88, 89, 101, 104, 105
merchant capitalist. *See* Yankee Trader
Molly Maguires, 46
Murray, Philip, 75, 76, 78, 83

National Industrial Recovery Act (NIRA), 65-66
National Labor Relations Act, 66
National Labor Relations Board (NLRB), 66, 96, 101
National Labor Union, 44
National Labor Union and Reform Party, 44-45

National Prohibition Act, 84, 85
National War Labor Board, 74, 75, 79
Norris-LaGuardia Act, 65

Oil Producing and Exporting Communities (OPEC), 92

Palmer, Mitchell, 57
political parties, workers', 43-44
Powderly, Terence V., 47, 48
Prohibition, 83-85
Protestant work ethic, 38

racketeering, 83-85
red scare, 57
Republic Steel, 69, 70
Reuther, Walter, 82, 83, 88-89, 104
right-to-work laws, 80-81
Rockefeller, John D., 24, 25
Roosevelt, Franklin Delano, 64-65, 73, 74, 75

scientific management, 62
Sedition Act, 56, 57
service industries, 93, 94, 101
slavery, 18, 34-35
steel industry, 60, 68-69, 70
Stephens, Uriah, 47
stock market crash, 63-64
strikes, 45-46, 58, 79, 80; by automobile workers, 70-71; by miners, 46, 58-60; by shoe workers, 45; by steel workers, 60-61, 69-70; by

textile workers, 54; first significant, 42; in colonial America, 15; injunctions against, 49-50, 65; sit-down, 69-70
Sylvis, William, 44

Taft-Hartley Act, 79-81
technology, changes in, 91-93
textile industry, 20, 30, 54, 93
trade associations, 10
Triangle Shirt Waist Factory fire, 21-22
Truman, Harry S, 79

unions. *See* labor unions
United Auto Workers (UAW), 88-89
United Mine Workers, 63, 66

United States Steel Corporation, 60, 71

Wagner Act, 66, 80
Wagner, Robert, 66
Walsh-Healy Act, 31
welfare capitalism, 62
Wobblies. *See* Industrial Workers of the World
workday, length of, 19, 42, 44, 47, 105
World War I, 37, 56, 57
World War II, 61, 71, 72-75, 78-79, 88

Yankee Trader, 11-12
yellow-dog contract, 51, 62

ACKNOWLEDGMENTS

The photographs and illustrations in this book are used courtesy of: Ford Motor Co., pp. 2, 61, 90; Women's Bureau, National Archives, p. 6; Library of Congress, pp. 9, 12, 14, 21, 30, 32, 41, 45, 47, 50, 53, 55 (bottom right), 65; The Mansell Collection, p. 10; Fresno City and County Historical Society Archives, p. 16; Labor Education Service, University of Minnesota, pp. 18, 102; Community Service Society, pp. 19, 29; Standard Oil Co., p. 24; Independent Picture Service, pp. 26, 48, 56, 98; New York Historical Society, New York, pp. 34, 35; Northern Pacific Railway, p. 37; Tamiment Institute Library, p. 44; Labor History Archives, Wayne State University, p. 55 (top); Chicago Historical Society, pp. 55 (bottom left), 70; National Archives, pp. 72, 75; AP/Wide World Photos, p. 59; The George Meany Memorial Archives, pp. 67, 74, 77; New York Public Library, p. 71; United Steelworkers of America, p. 78; AFL-CIO, pp. 82, 105; State Photographic Archives, Strozier Library, Florida State University, p. 84; Peter Marcus, p. 87; Chase Ltd., p. 89; UPI/Bettmann Newsphotos, p. 92; Mitsubishi Motors Corporation, p. 94; John Madere, p. 95; Minnesota Orchestra, p. 99 (top); Charles Coushman, p. 99 (bottom).

Front cover photograph courtesy of John Madere. Back cover photograph courtesy of Labor Education Service, University of Minnesota.